THE GREENHOUSE

THE
GREENHOUSE

poems

LISA GLUSKIN STONESTREET

Winner of the 2014 Frost Place Chapbook Competition

DURHAM, NORTH CAROLINA

THE GREENHOUSE

Copyright © 2014 by Lisa Gluskin Stonestreet

———————

Winner of the 2014 Frost Place Chapbook Competition
Selected by David Baker

———————

Published in the United States of America

Library of Congress Cataloging-in-Publication Data

Stonestreet, Lisa Gluskin
The Greenhouse: poems / by Lisa Gluskin Stonestreet
p.   cm.
ISBN-13: 978-1-4243-1802-5 (Paperback)

Book design by Flying Hand Studio

———————

Published by Bull City Press
1217 Odyssey Drive
Durham, NC 27713

www.BullCityPress.com

CONTENTS

for Truman

Like That

The first time
            I leaned over and swept the tip of my smallest fingernail down into

the whorl of your ear *(bigger than your elbow)*, and you yelped
in violation:
                        forgive me

it is no longer my ear
                    (little boat, little shell I carved)

flushing pink, even now, at the embarrassment, the *satisfaction*—

sliver-moon of yellow wax:
                        tiny victory.

. . .

Lovers say, *I did not know*

where my body ended and yours began.
I did not know. Even yesterday when you laughed,

reared back, your head
                    quick-snap against my upper lip, both of us

laughing and then me still laughing, eye-sting, drop of blood
at the crown of your head, panic—

                        oh, *mine*. This morning

holding, rough/soft, drawing my tongue
up under my lip, compelling—

                        Like that.

And entirely unlike, of course

               (*of course*, we must say, feel we must say)—

. . .

Six months until you crawled, the only calm
lay in your being tied
           to me—head up, bumping my ribs,

head up, eyes open, that same position
on my body that you took inside it

           (the acupuncture, the headstands: what I wouldn't do
           in those last weeks to turn you toward the earth—)

and everything slipping, permeable,   you/me
the least of it:

      day/night   inside/outside   body/body

what I wouldn't do

        (I could open the door)

wait: wavering Jewish atheist that I am—

           I *made* you.

Flowers, Doggies, the Moon

It's only beginning to recede, that time, that milk-
    dream

            of a year

the long hours in the rocker, the occasional calculating, to assuage my restlessness,
    its portion: that is, the first of his/the last

        of my thirties: one year. One percent, two? Worth so much
        more, I think (once more)
                        and so once more keep

rocking, switch sides, watch

the last streetcars lumbering home through the half-open blinds, switch sides, brief flicker
    at the corner of his mouth, a sigh, rocking...

        (and where else would I rather be?)

That's not to call up the rhetoric of choice, privilege, the drill
    of tussling generations (*what we fought for / what we take for granted*

and embrace): it's just
        so difficult to step (back) into that sea, soft swirl without counting—

        only to rise, days later,

                in a different spot on the waves.

. . .

What did you do today?

Check the mommy-memoirs: nurse, bathe, dress, change, sleep, fail to sleep; feel about it

     all the ways one is supposed, or not supposed, to feel—

                    in the beginning, though, we were

free even of the balm of naming:

          flowers, doggies, the moon

on its pages or in the sky. Only circles within circles, and doing, or even feeling, so much
       beside the point: the warm thrum of the tide.

. . .

Once I tried sitting—this, when my life was one quietly perfectible room, discipline,
books and tea, a long view of hills and the signal tower—driving to the zendo in morning
frost and folding my legs on a square white mat.

How impossible it was, first sending each thought out on its little line

    (boat / boat / boat)

then the fidgeting, the sarcasm, sudden aches; then finally reduced to counting back from
a hundred, and still the harbor with its jostling and its tethers—

38, 38, 38—

    37—

. . .

Isn't this one idea of heaven? beyond
giving, or change, or love and down

into this deep bright sphere of what-is, tomorrow
       and yesterday lost in eddy of *here*—

the only count the heartbeat rhythm of his mouth
       (small round callus on the upper lip) and us together back and forth in the chair—

. . .

How can you have memory without language my friend asks, one of those
many slow mornings, and even then the thought flows back into the sea, a place
sans both ten o'clock and tomorrow: present, present, present—

our two boys nursing, again, sometime midafternoon and a wave laps at the rug, each of us
bobbing cross-legged and curled over,

       bowless hulls for our swaddled sons.

. . .

Is this why we remember nothing of the time? Its only position *before*.

Memory without language. Memory of face, smell. The bath, the big dog, the tree.
But mostly of this:

       no name, no category. Milk.

       The present nudging at the shore.

. . .

He is asleep and I'm awake.

My husband and I joke: what's a good dream for a baby?

      The breast.

Bad dream?

      No breast.

But seriously, folks: An eternity of no breast.

. . .

38, 38, 38, 37—

and sometimes it is all I can do. Calling up the masks of patience, again.

. . .

(nurse, bathe, dress, change, sleep, fail to sleep; feel about it)

. . .

Walking, rocking. Singing one song when all the rest have fled from memory:
      oatmeal, oatmeal, it's a meal made of oats. Oatmeal, oatmeal—

      [Repeat until the space between the blinds goes violet, white.]

. . .

Even out there, the lines get tangled. Especially out there. Each hull
      throwing out a line to the next, a web, a path back to not-

here, not-now, back on the shore

of the phone call, the gas bill, the poem and how it should end, the need

to show up tethered to the tug on the other end: and it's so easy to see myself hopping from
one to the next, to link them like metaphor until all the clocks line up on either side and the
kitchen and the desk are sparkling empty, arrayed

      (not now / not now / not now)

scows pulling out, laden—

. . .

      —rock, switch sides, watch

for the slow dip of eyelid, the open hand. He's beginning
      to fight it, swimming up for one more round

      (Eye. Eyebrow. Nose. Mouth! Teeth, teeth—)

      of saying, and the moon on the waves is a moon in the book, the book

we read yesterday, in the big chair at the window, and the eye under its brow

      is round like the moon; the lines multiply, shimmer
      in the light of the day, of *this morning* and *what we're doing tomorrow* and

now we're again down in it: his eye a crescent slipping into line

        and on the horizon the dozen tiny hulls receding, receding, going to silhouette
        as we're pulled together

            back into the mute night sea—

Baby / Honey

DO NOT FEED TO INFANTS UNDER ONE YEAR OF AGE

1.

It does help, the Internet, the constellations

of data, so much of it leaving one feeling even more so

than before (alien: as in stranger on this planet), but still/but then

the echoing array

of *yes, me too* some days small balm and others

pure drug, sucked up in desperation and binge, endless catalog

of possibilities

       (scared to fall asleep in the rocker with the baby in her arms)

       (scared to walk by the upstairs railing because she feared tripping and tossing the baby over)

       (scared of measuring out the insulin incorrectly)

       (scared that she would walk out the door and down to the bar)

and yet/and so

paralysis of possible fates

              x carved into your ankle, antidote for snakebite

2.

Botulism? Really?

            (deliberate step past the top of the stairs)

3.

That patch at the back of his ear: dirt and peanut butter and chlorine and milk

when it feels like too much, my friend says, *I try to remember to look at their hands*

swarm circling the wild cherry in the yard

chopping apples for the new year

how we go about each day, how we ever get beyond
that one square inch of skin

4.

Millions of babies, of mothers, millions more jars

flowing from the conveyor belt. Labels in all caps, black
on white on gold.

Attencion. Mis en garde.

Chimera

Microchimerism is the persistent presence of a few genetically distinct cells in an organism … cells containing the male Y chromosome were found circulating in the blood of women after pregnancy.

I want them out. I want
to be myself, my self
again. My old untethered,

young untied. I lie: I want

nothing more—or want
no more the point.
Dendritic, en-

twined, signed on
for the duration. Bright
tangle, snaking line

of fire. The crucible

does not ask
for want. Is. Tied in,
shot through. Fired.

What I Taught Him

in sitting next to the high chair, half-
hearing, half *hmmm*— that part
the part dog-earing a page, cracking

a spine (book arrived in the mail, life-raft

                in its yellow envelope)

stealing bites of his apple, half-eye
on the table of contents

                a wondrous disease
                (or its inoculation)

half here in the kitchen

                (& while nursing)
                (& on the train)
                (&)
                (&)

the insistence, the sound (the subway under the avenues, the hum
of insects even on the meadow even at night, even those nights

                I'd once woken

because of the quiet, something to the left
of the audible spectrum—sound

that is not a sound, sound that clung to me   even once the new person
washed out of me, long after

his body was no longer made from mine, when he was routinely
miles away, miles

or hundreds of miles) and in the dark

of the meadow over the one mountain
I was the one making the sound, it was   a transponder a circuit a circle

at each station a boost and so
now, daily, still:

                                        receptor, antennae.
                                        Walking around the city at a certain frequency.

The part underlining in the margin.
The part chewing on the corners. The part licking at the paper cut on the lip.
Hungry pulling and digging, battery needing the charge, spark

                                        needing the flint,

comfort of the smell, escape and compulsion,
the self that I was, the source of the surge:

                                        the book the book the book.

and now in the kitchen, bodily here/half-
gone, crumbs across the tray and ten o'clock
and sticky sunlight on the wood

                                        (present)
                                        (& while pulling back into the present)
                                        (& while sending and receiving)

and offering another half-bite and his red pajama top with the trains
on it and I'm holding down the page with one hand and cutting up
apple with the other, split

> (insistent)
> (yielding)
> (pulled)
>
>
> (hanging on)

After Dropping My Son Off at Preschool

The world slowly coming back. The luxury of stepping outside

myself
> *where is outside?*
> *rehearsing for years now*

I was a bubble, a greenhouse, a lens—

> clear, like water, present like water, spreading, reflecting
> ratcheting down the viewfinder

> self being a place encompassing a small boy

Step outside yourself, ma'am, and no one will get hurt

> Nobody got hurt, not seriously.
> It's a goddamn miracle.

. . .

The world is mine for six hours.

> Newspapers! I could read

a newspaper. I have the luxury, the privilege.

I mention this only
to get it out of the way.

. . .

Pedicure, they say. *Money-market account.*
Pilates. New York Times. Organic tomatoes. LLC.

Are you writing again?

. . .

The gingko is dropping leaves on the sidewalk in front of the coffee shop.

I want to have deep thoughts about this.

The gingko is the most ancient of trees.
I think I made that up. No, I Googled it. No—

                  It is a luxury and a privilege to be such an idiot.

. . .

self being a place:

       the greenhouse encompassing three things: a mother, a gingko tree, a boy.

He is always there. Now there are seven or eight toy vehicles there as well. He has framed,
with his father's help, the leaf of the gingko—full and red, two blushing lobes—and hung it
on his wall, at eye level.

The leaves accumulate, in my pockets, the glove compartment, along the back edge of my desk.
Some of the leaves make it into collages. Some are given names: Henry, Alice, Bizzo. Mr. Zzbz.
Some are ground under the wheels of the cars, which also have names.

. . .

Plotted and planned and tracked and graphed and still
it came suddenly, fogged the evil eye with its emerald swoon.

The curving mire, the back-in-ness, rounded vowels
through a scrim? a screen? Seeped in that blood, recircled, recycled—

No heaven, I thought, *other than this*. And:

                    please God, just ten minutes to pee.

. . .

This is my job, and I am more than ready for it and I am not ready for it and what supplies have I
packed for your journey? Water bottle, sunscreen, hats for sun and cold. Snacks from the Japanese
grocery. Extra socks in a ziploc bag.

. . .

and oh there is yet one
part of me that breathes in and out
at a quicker pace, that smaller hotter
heart

. . .

Dropoff, pickup. The prescription, the renewal, the calls and clients.
The days with their windows, rusty levers cranked open.

. . .

I am back in the coffee shop, three months later, four? The gingko a pale green. I think
this is where the metaphor breaks down.

                              At night now,
two stories, three. I rub his back, inhale— a more complex loam. I step around
toy cars, the animals arrayed in sentry against the dark.

Open the door, close it quietly, and the night
                              opens up its hours, a few more, a few more—

Called

and I go

down into it, the hall again
(streetlights, blinds)

all the same all the dark

down into it and do what must be done
with my body, with the patience
that I do not have

fellow sufferer, fellow sleeper, not-

sleeper, seeker

night boat, little sail

in the slow air in the rounded dark
inside the broken night

rudderless   elliptical

in the stitched-together minute

minute

minute

365 x night x 8   (new)

x 4
x 2
x 8 again   (despair, iron)
x 2

x 1, x occasional, x rarity (fever, monsters, light)

= now

= again

once

Anchor

I believed I could make it up, that *will*
was *power*, not in that greasy
philosophy-boy way but in the ancient sense

of generosity of making: a poem or a meal
or perhaps a practice (I like that, just flexing
the fingers—)

        Why do I keep returning
to that room, the scarred stone Buddha
above the radiator, desk and chair,
mirror of tarnished gilt and the rules
did not apply. It helped

             that they were such small rules:
art and finance and the hum of the freeway
at the bottom of the hill. One window that opened.

One thing can be made. Or kept, for a while.
If it wasn't something, it would be
something else. A doubling of cells. Lucky, lucky,

and eventually bad luck too (category: body.
category: money. category: middle-class
artists, global collapse, blow to the head: the tired usual,

the highwire and the blessed net). And lucky
even out of that, wolf like a wind at the door.

About that doubling: We made a person,
anchor to the earth. Lucky boy.

So like I said you do the one step
tra-la see how it's done and look up to find
you are being pulled by something bigger, the hand

of some giant clock, have in fact
lashed yourself to it with great joy—

and it split me open, made me
pure triage:

       will such a flimsy ticket

More, Again (Poppies)

There is popcorn all over the rug. Do you want

me to tell that story? Because almost guaranteed you will find
it boring
        (domestic) (female) (too much) (too little, too small)

Check one. Move on. Too bad: You will find

pieces for weeks, in the couch, constellation
of explosion, brittle gold against the blue, glint and scatter

visible only in the light of the screen, another night with the same bowl, another way
to make it from 6 to 8, 7 to 9,

the schedules, the negotiation, teeth brushed or un-,
clean sheets, a quick pass over everything
                good enough: or maybe it's enough

to make you want a night of your own, everyone
piled cozily in among the crumbs—

. . .

Dorothy, meanwhile, is nodding down, accretion in the rows and that one falling,
lost and happy, for once, to let it go, to release
just for a minute the demands of narrative and celluloid, just sleep,
                       just step

out of the second act and into this cradle,
more than she has ever seen, *so quiet*—

                                        the heavy red heads, blanket opening up
                                        under the pinkening sky.

And in the backstory, turn of the hourglass,
our heroes hindered and threatened from afar:

                              even if you are not sleeping you are still dying

That's story, though, *off into the sunset*
is a direction isn't it, off into the flat of the screen…

meanwhile, meanwhile, every spark in the sky falling, plot moving
inexorably forward, oh my darlings if we could only lie down and rest, stop the spinning, the trickle

of sand, the dust and dust again and then the washing and the sleeping and then again to bed

                              stilled in the fields of our slumber—

. . .

And now, and still. Child sleeping sprawled out, missing the march
to the castle, winged monkeys gathering on the horizon.

Many water, he used to say. Or *one, two, many*.

Dysnomia

They say it comes back, it always   comes back—
run the rebuilt _____ round the track

      {lacuna}

noun, dropped down the rabbithole:
the door, the lock, the lack, the line, the time
                     the mind.

Here's where a good vocabulary comes in handy.

pop in the placeholder, bravado of the dropped
                     call. Stop. Don't
stop. Stooped.

      That was a typo, not my brain.

Slipped. Stripped.

(run around it? pull out
         another slip. Another riff.)

The tester and I walk down a long hall, chatting. Linoleum.
Cheery posters. I'm a good test-taker. Conversationalist.
Raised to please. Born to run. Sunday *New York Times*
for fun, for fun.

. . .

Name as many things as you can that start with S.
Start. Star. Son. Sun.

Stop.

Stop?

Mind the gap. Mind the.

Mind.

Very superior. Superior. High normal. Normal. _____. (What was it called?

Below that.) The drop-spike in the chart. Gears locking, falling

                                    out and through.

Left frontal. White matter. Matters, what matters,

                              mattering. Nattering.

                              Something that was. Off the rails.

. . .

Mattering. While others stop to think, it is impolite to:

  (a) fidget

  (b) interrupt

  (c) summarize.

Raised to please. Politeness is difficult, regardless. The rabbit
has to go somewhere. It takes up some amount of space.
It likes to run.

In the margin of the book, repeat the cue:

S   L   O   W   D   O   W   N

The nouns. Through the trap door, it feels, it seems

but seems = theory, really

                              (or in the new theory)

it is the retrieval mechanism that is faulty: the hinge perhaps, the gap, the space
between wires, spark circling and pooling.

Omega 3s, Bs and Ds. Gingko biloba, willow.

Blueberries, chocolate, sleep.

The dictionary a palace of shelves, each shelf a litany of jars.

                    Mind the gap.
                    Leap the track.

Rabbit, rabbit, rabbit.

Charge

(When the giant sacrifices himself for the boy)

                      (and on the screen

the men marching toward him   all the pieces

                            falling from his metal body

steaming in the snow)

When the giant sacrifices himself for the boy, the boy

at my side is lifted for a moment,

                   filled with air, the intake, the stop-

gasp held aloft, no sound:

             the shock at the top of the arc, the drop—

and only then, on the way down, opens into sob: hard water

wrung from a knot. All the pieces

                  falling.

Small hot forehead pressed to my chest. Animal exposed in the storm.

Knows himself then, knows himself to want more.

Anchor

And if I put down my book to read him a book
and if I put down that book to check the mail
and if I put down the mail to get up and brush my hair

and make pancakes (because it is Saturday
and I have promised pancakes) and if, in measuring the flour,
I hold it up to the light to check the level

                                        (because I want

to be more accurate) and if all this happens entirely
in my head because I am still in actuality
trying to get myself out of bed, and

                        oh I am so sick of the self:

hauling it around everywhere, dragging it along even as my brain
chases the tail of another dangling modifier in a sentence
without a subject, that is

                        without an anchor, even as everything here

is an anchor: the shell of the brush, the scarred griddle,
my son's feet pushing into the warm space behind my knees,
my husband's arm behind my head, tangled ballast
nudging our raft out into the day.

                        I used to worry I'd float straight up
off the earth, snap my tether, fear and relief, I was 20, it was all meaningful
weather: flame & snow.

                Now the self is a turtle
on a rope, prehistoric pull-toy heavy as a station wagon

with compartments for water and sunglasses.

                              Sometimes I forget myself

and leave it in the garage. Sometimes I ride it around so it doesn't get lonely.

Sometimes it drifts off down a tributary and we go sailing on,

three of us in our big bed. It thinks it's steering

                              but it's not.

NOTES & ACKNOWLEDGMENTS

"Chimera": The epigraph is from a 2012 *Scientific American* article entitled "Scientists Discover Children's Cells Living in Mothers' Brains." From the article: "This condition is called chimerism after the fire-breathing Chimera from Greek mythology, a creature that was part serpent, part lion, and part goat. Naturally occurring chimeras are far less ominous, though, and include such creatures as the slime mold and corals."

"Dysnomia": The title refers to a difficulty recalling or inability to recall words, especially nouns.

———————

Thanks to the journals where the following poems appeared, often in slightly different form:

At Length: "Flowers, Doggies, the Moon"
Cream City Review: "Like That," What I Taught Him," "After Dropping My Son
                Off at Preschool," Dysnomia," "Anchor" (*And if I put down my book…*)
Edge: "More, Again (Poppies)," "Baby/Honey"
Kenyon Review Online: "Anchor" (*I believed I could make it up…*)

Many thanks to David Baker, for choosing this manuscript, and to Ross White and everyone at Bull City Press; every writer should be so lucky as to have an editor as thoughtful, funny, and dedicated as Ross. To Patrick Donnelly, Maudelle Driskell, Sarah Audsley, and everyone at the Frost Place Poetry Seminar for the invitation, encouragement, and opportunity that the prize, and the place, allow.

Thanks to all the fellow travelers, tied together in the real and virtual worlds, who help me remember that what we do matters: The Warren Wilson community, especially the Wallygoats, for feasts both metaphorical and literal. 13 Ways, without whom I might never actually finish anything. The Aurora community, for giving my son a place to be himself. The Moxites, for giving my mother-self the same. Debra, who has read the story from the beginning and still wants to know what will happen next. Truman, who changed everything. And Erich, who so often in those years was on the shore, waving as we rowed out, then in again. Who was the shore we rowed home to. Who anchored, and anchors, us now.

ABOUT THE AUTHOR

LISA GLUSKIN STONESTREET's *Tulips, Water, Ash* was selected for the Morse Poetry Prize. Her poems have been awarded a Javits Fellowship and a Phelan Award, and have appeared in journals including *At Length*, *Blackbird*, *Cream City Review*, *The Iowa Review*, *Kenyon Review*, and *Quarterly West* and in the anthologies *Best New Poets* and *The Bloomsbury Anthology of Contemporary Jewish American Poetry*. She writes, edits, and teaches in Oakland, California.